BEFORE THE DESIRE TO EAT

poems by

R. Stempel

Finishing Line Press
Georgetown, Kentucky

BEFORE THE DESIRE TO EAT

Copyright © 2022 by R. Stempel
ISBN 978-1-64662-787-5 First Edition
All rights reserved under International and Pan-American Copyright Conventions. No part of this book may be reproduced in any manner whatsoever without written permission from the publisher, except in the case of brief quotations embodied in critical articles and reviews.

ACKNOWLEDGMENTS

"There Are Too Many Bird Metaphors" appears in *dreams walking*, Issue 4
"Running Late for My Kitchen Soliloquy" appears in *Seiren Quarterly*, Issue 2
"Affirmation Exercise" appears in *Pinwheel Journal*, Issue 18
"Benny Facetimes Me from Titlow Beach While She Smokes a Fat Joint" appears in *the Under Review*, Issue 2
"Good Bone" appears in *2River View*, Issue 25.2
"HOMEBODY VLOG / THE ALL-GIRLS DREAM" appears in *The Comments Section*, Issue 1

Publisher: Leah Huete de Maines
Editor: Christen Kincaid
Cover Art and Design: R. Stempel
Author Photo: Robin Gow

Order online: www.finishinglinepress.com
also available on amazon.com

Author inquiries and mail orders:
Finishing Line Press
PO Box 1626
Georgetown, Kentucky 40324
USA

Table of Contents

There Are Too Many Bird Metaphors 1

Running Late For My Kitchen Soliloquy 2

Appetizers 3

Affirmation Exercise 4

Ode to Crock-Pot 5

Off-Menu 6

Poultry 7

Benny Facetimes Me from Titlow Beach While She Smokes
 a Fat Joint 13

If Every Trashcan Had a Lid I Wouldn't Need To Be Here 14

A Banana Tastes Like Nail Polish 16

Guilt/Gelt 17

Rehomed Gefilte Fish 18

Whistleblowers of the Valley 19

FARM TO TABLE 21

Good Bone 22

What Is Above an Oven of This Proportion? 23

Calories Burnt in Death Rattle 24

The Butcher Courts a Bull Dyke 25

HOMEBODY VLOG / THE ALL-GIRLS DREAM 26

*but see how hideous hearse-shined my feathers,
see my wings spread like a dead book of legs,
see my brutal beak a seed-thief in the club light.*

—*sam sax*

There Are Too Many Bird Metaphors

under a petri dish sky I understand all meaning
is constructed to be deconstructed

a diagonal frame isolates, names
something outside common

for researchers to arrange their tongues
like feathers, aim for flight

aim for grayscale dust bunnies &
harvest *predator* from the uncanny

fingers of a not-quite-eagle
or a maybe-raven—

forgive me, reader, for the connection;
I know there are so many.

Running Late For My Kitchen Soliloquy

The antipasto's lacking
in vinegar, my favorite food
group. A first date is like
vinegar—fructose rotting
smells like bacterial vaginosis:
ammonia, not fish.

I said *A first date is like vinegar*
& like a good man, you don't
respond. You spit pearls
anywhere they'll fit.

Over shellfish I say
I'm wrongly allergic
& offer an undesirable adage—

the rotary phone was built to withstand a good fingering.
Not me.

Over dessert you question my daily nomenclature.
I respond *We all could use new names* & offer no follow-up
but too many Tic-Tacs.

Appetizers

Arguably I'm in love
with all my friends. It feels sneaky

when I, arms widened, perform
palatial, baiting

my beauties under guise
of something less carnal. I

catch my tongue, a gamey meat behind
fabric trenches, just in time—

I'm a mongrel bred to court,
fermenting sweet talk to bury

beneath mouth-bone. We all have
mouth-bone real estate & for this reason

I'll anchor in anyone, trigger
an underused salivary gland, bathe

in the wet heat of a *what if* & lend
myself to combustion: I,

a ginger cough-drop too
bitter to swallow, seek to

suppress appetite for any other. Too
few are taught this

iteration of Eden doesn't
protect. An electric fence is an electric fence

only in name & I've never been
much of an electrician. You wouldn't

believe how many girls go for that first
course like another won't follow.

Affirmation Exercise

Seven praying mantises playing martyr before the desire to eat flickers its
fight. They all look
the same. Syrupy strings glue fork to midnight, envelop the kitchen table to
find an excuse

        like, this will make me a bad mother.

We catch on the third night, the moon following. I am rich & untouchable
I fuck three failed praxes: man is hell   mantis hell   man's a helluva hole-
chaser

        & tell them, *Tell me the good reds to soak in.*

Seven wayward sons worry tumescent bug bites to crescendo in white. I
disgust myself sometimes with these reductions.

Ode to Crock-Pot

Gestational brine cures my own
pig heart in Egyptian salts & capers.
Nothing now can spoil my hollows
where once like on Mars
there were rivers.

My pig heart atrophies,
its mannish branches spew bile
I'll keep in bone china teacups
my grandmother will gift me
if & only if I can land a man

but the one she envisions is already married!

Nothing a low flame can't soften she says
& I tend to agree.

An alluvial valley forms in waiting
& God, do I wait! for an *us*
shaped by water in some form,
slow-cooked like pork shoulder.

The man my grandmother envisions,
a pork shoulder himself, the strings bound
tight, their gridlines browning
now, glowing…

I get away with murder in porcelain

so for lunch I use my father's credit card to buy gummy worms & kombucha.

Off-Menu

I babysit the trash bins with her best
translations—her, this house, she buzzes
& the buzzing won't cease but is so slight
I wonder if I'm her only listener.
The garbage man would be out of a job
if my neuroses found other outlets.
I caulk walls with honeyed
saliva & drain electric to breathe
wattage through hickory'd meat.
I take the form of a weapon prospered against me.
But the buzzing! how much can she eat!

Poultry
    (Or: Crystal Lil, in pectore)

1.

I've been snorting expired fabric softener to cope with a recent salmonella diagnosis. In chunks it stumbles from the box like the basement has its own rules of gravity. I've tried widening the factory-perforated hole to no avail; the chunks fall out with as much hesitation. I crush them with my fat thumb, flatten each to its primordial form in pulver. I have to be quick—maybe the excitement?—finger oil or sweat mattes them into thick pucks I wouldn't dare inhale in whole. I don't have a death wish, only Nausea!

    Everything in moderation. Only once a day, maybe twice if I'm feeling frisky—throbbing sinuses belittle the digestive virus into submission. Head pain is less shameful, borders on sympathetic. Better this on the record than the truth—I still have the feathers in my teeth!

2.

The Taconic is a dangerous highway. Two lanes, narrow & flanked by long stretches of vegetation hiccuped into disorienting repetition. When the curve strikes
                                         & it does strike
there's a moment of panic or relief. In that moment death
comes from the left: driver's side to driver's side in quantum tango 'til maybe God gives
you the lead & you bow out in time.

You are in a small car with a horn high-pitched & *fruity* like your first boyfriend.

You are in a small car & the bird in question is now embedded in the front tires.

You christen it *foie gras* but today you will go hungry.

3.

My sister presents a dinner spread on Fridays full of fodder like our family's not big enough already. My disgust of consumption is an afterthought & I eat that, too. It doesn't go down as easy as schmaltz. I'm getting fat again & my sister is *living* for it. I leave grease stains on diary pages & jeans leave their kiss marks on love handles.

I lock myself in the bathroom, sit fully clothed in the bathtub & listen to my sister's voice explain the refining process for goose fat to our dad who's definitely not listening, who's definitely fucking his coworker who's young & hot & vegan & doesn't eat goose fat.

When I come back out I feel better than before knowing that my sister is willing ugliness for the wrong girl. I feel better but I've not had my fill. I say we should try a vegan Shabbos.

My dad, a terrible liar, is picking the tendony bits from his teeth with his thumbnail when his mouth snaps down. He yelps like an inbred pup & my sister starts to cry.

This is the final blow. This is neither fit nor proper.

4.

Pigeon chicks look like caricatures of old Jewish men, look like my husband. My husband works in squab husbandry so he always smells delectable. Sometimes he brings me the still-feathered bits discarded after a slaughter & I cook pigeon pie for us & feel okay with loving him. In the interim, time I only measure as in between pigeon pies, my ears ring *l'appel du vide* without respite. I drive to the A&P-turned-Key Food, the one further away that caters to our town's white trash fringe, offering nearly expired meats & produce for counterfeit food stamps. It's not the real thing, but it'll do.

My husband who works in squab husbandry would be embarrassed to know I shop at this further away Key Food but he's gone to work for the week or the month & I am alone with my thoughts & bloody chicken breasts, large & muscular enough to imagine they're still pulsing. A chicken is no red junglefowl so its blood tastes leaden when I lap it up. I make myself laugh from the thought of my husband walking in on me. I love a good laugh & later I love my husband when he brings home a fresh kill.

5.

An executive chef scrapes his taste buds off every weekday morning with a meat cleaver, Damascus steel. He does this so he can give exclusively positive feedback & remain objective. He does this so he can stomach his wife's cooking. He does this so he can savor his mistress's cock.

His sous-chef is reading My Mistress's Sparrow is Dead & the executive chef can't decide if that's a threat or premonition. He runs it by his mistress who says *It's probably both* then lifts her negligee to release four turtle doves. They scramble from beneath satin folds with impressive gusto, unaware their wings are clipped. When they drop they ram their wooden beaks into the floor.

Well? prompts his mistress.

He proceeds to lift each of the four turtle doves gently into the light, cradling their tiny necks against his index finger before forcing his thumb upwards. The fourth *snap* sends them both into ecstasy. The fourth snap sends a fifth turtle dove from between his mistress's thighs. This one isn't clipped. This one heads straight for his left eye.

That's not right! his mistress apologizes, like she's rehearsed.

This one causes the executive chef to lament his love of all birds.

6.

You can't talk about horse sex like that on TV anymore I say to no one in particular. I am seated on an old couch that smells like ass or dog with my father who forgot my birthday. We're watching Johnny Carson reruns & in this episode he makes a joke about racehorse semen.

Really, you can't talk about horse sex like that on TV anymore.

My dad says he doesn't get it, he doesn't think the joke's sexual in nature. He doesn't see the sex, really, in anything. That's why mom left him.

A woman can satisfy every permutation of man, but a two-way street is hard to find Mom told me before she left for the Pacific Northwest to conduct research for what she brands a New Age anthropology.

In her latest email, she tells me she's six-months deep in data on infidelity & the L.L. Bean lesbian.

She writes *Their species is young & hot & vegan, three things I aspire to be.*

My dad says he's going to bed & between me, the dog, & Johnny Carson, I feel the most at home.

Before my dad retires, he says he's left a bag of Mom's lingerie by the pantry, tells me I can look through & keep what I want. I know this is both his way of telling me he doesn't see me as his son & that he's grateful for my resourcefulness.

I'll take a look after I feed the turtle doves.

Benny Facetimes Me from Titlow Beach
While She Smokes a Fat Joint

& I hesitate to receive   the past week I'm more of myself
                                                than ever
I stare   at my reflection for eleven
                                    uninterrupted minutes & decide
this place, my childhood home   became a different person

a cul-de-sac   a radiator squeal   or a more concrete *other*—
                            it reached refiguration
before my return!   I don't like to be predated.
                I want the seven-year cell-
cycle shortened to seconds—don't you?

I want a universal rebranding
                    every breath a creator & destroyer. I tell Benny
I'm expanding   & it's neither good nor bad but in retrospect
                    I may have said nothing.
I retreat to the mirror, press myself into the pane
                                        will my flesh

to ectoplasm   reclaim athleticism for a new age where
                        my viscera's self-sufficient &
to eat is obsolete   where I see my body
                                as lithe & sprung, like
a Sharapova   or a Kournikova
            but here & now I'm no   jasmine-footed deity

I'm a bloodhound   groomed to bury
        I'm a 3-am resolution of sound   & sound-off!
a tennis court appears below my bedroom window
                Benny says she can see it, too.
Benny says, *You dig a hole in the ground.*
                    You bury the bones   *not yourself.*

If Every Trashcan Had a Lid I Wouldn't Need To Be Here

Here
is a female
living space
      is floral illusion

Here
I hide uneaten
breakfasts
wrapped neatly
in newsprint

Later, I comb through
a January 1969 Playboy
to comb past
zaftig
      & seep
into the role

Practice girlish,
look for my best
angles

Hold static
a near-yellow smile,
head titled
in a symmetry
I'm too young
to grasp

Hold static—
wait
for a hiccup
      & spill:

foamy vomit

Ignore the
too red color—

it's a flame,
the nature of the beast
is throwing soot

Taste absolutes:
marmalades & preserves
from the uncanny valley

Feel like a set
of intestines:
twenty-two feet long
& velvet-lined
like the heart-
shaped bed
of a honeymoon
suite fit for
a centerfold

A Banana Tastes Like Nail Polish

You are dead from the neck down, your heart a black grape.
This is a poem. This is a critical conversation about motherhood.

You are a vague pronoun, you write
murder & underline it
four times

then, six hysterias later—

Do you want to be a chef or a balloon?
(the difference might surprise you!)

This is what happens sans supervision. Get together
your best girl-scraps & tell your wrists to breathe

        black grape   black grape   black grape   (vague)

Forgive me while I wax poetic (I haven't looked at you
all morning)   Do you want to be a chef or a balloon?

For chef, remember the parts of a baby—
too small.

Forgive me while I wax poetic—
I am in search of a bitter omen.

I'm versatile this way.

For balloon, best to eat before helium   (chef not necessary)

Forgive me but this banana tastes like nail polish.

Guilt/Gelt

I don't speak in aphorisms but I refuse
to believe the pomegranate. I've never been
breastfed, so its crowned nipple-stem
does nothing for me. The pomegranate
bleeds in poetry—or was it poverty?—
as does the beet but I'm sick of Slavic
accusations. The pomegranate's blood, bitter
water, promises sweet permission. A Holy
not Higher than Holiest, the pomegranate debuts
at a distance not exotic
but strange not *strange*
fruit though
we love to make the connection. I refuse
to believe the pomegranate when it shakes
its cellulose jungle-gym, holding on to
rattler coinage. Do we know if we can eat them,
if the body digests hard   or lets it pass
undisturbed? How much is undisturbed
in passage? I refuse to believe the pomegranate
whose skin won't peel.

Rehomed Gefilte Fish

The fish that is kosher is covered
in visible scales, easily plucked
like the eczema of the old
Jewish man from five poems ago.

Does the fishmonger know
who poaches their spines?
Forcemeat is porous like
pumice but somehow less
appetizing than meatloaf, tastes not
like the ocean but sick
seawater.

I've never had meatloaf
but that's not to say I don't enjoy it
with a teaspoon of fat-
free milk—I thank the farmer for this—

anything is enjoyable, even
my mother. Even a dinner
abundantly dead, burning in
horseradish   blood-dark like
nail polish.

Whistleblowers of the Valley

Baby teeth arranged in chronological order, the oral valleys
they leave behind keep heads buoyant, asking to be stuffed like stockings.
Archives of this nature define for a husband what is premium
against their wives' better judgment. The wives solicit severance
in inarticulate voice-memos. Briefly,
a husband will comply if & only if an orgy of seafood

waits tableside. But the wives learn to repurpose the sea,
& where they're going—note: a trench is a valley—
crustaceans come shell-less, come begging for raw beheading.
The wives slip into serpentine molds, scaly stockings
they took from their underaged daughters when they left. *Severance*
they explain *starts with cotton & elastic.* Their premium

price-tags weigh them down, bind them in premium
fish net—some bondage can't be avoided. The husbands, hovering, see food
in the net, not realizing their wives left behind little love tokens, severed
doll parts drenched in girl-blood. The valley
collects wives like a husband's mouth-hole collects dust his stocky
hands fail to sweep. Only wives know not to sweep but to blow

in whistles. A whistle is a palette cleanser: brief
but no small undertaking. Beneath the surface the wives find preemies
unfettered to cord. The wives knit stockings
from kelp, ask the manta ray if he can recommend the seafood
alternative to breastfeeding. The manta ray says *This valley
rejects alternatives, exists purely in hypotheticals.* Severe

is the warning of the manta ray. Severe
are the reactions of the wives who in panic swallow the preemies, break
& utter prayers as their unformed skulls compress under pressure in the
    valley.
The manta ray has a cautionary tale for filicide: *The premium
bounty targets the consumer of seafood.*
The wives protest in anger & fear, pull their kelp-stockings

taut. The manta ray, like any man, lusts after a stocking
stretched to completion, offers his own bit of severance:
Let me swallow you like krill. The wives cry *We're not seafood!*
but the manta ray, bemused, knows they are wives below

the scale-belt, entertains charging their husbands for a prime-
time show. The manta ray, bemused, knows the market in the valley

will sell its stock in wives to the highest bidder,
& the wives without a savior will gouge their eyes with prism
suncatchers. When men see food, they eat it. That's not unique to the valley.

FARM TO TABLE

A therapist's office surrounded by exoskeleton gaudy gold & crimson. An empty office chair whispers palindromes. FARMER & PIG sit too close & caked in flour, sieve their own chalk outlines.

PIG sitting upright, her gaze remains on FARMER. FARMER sits, his legs apart, staring at the audience, cradling his comically large rifle.

PIG: I think you're getting a-head of yourself.

FARMER: I've never been anywhere else.

PIG: I don't understand.

FARMER: You don't need to for it to be the case.

PIG: I want to understand.

FARMER: It's not important. Not at all.

PIG: She's late.

FARMER: We're early.

PIG: Not early enough.

FARMER: It's not important.

PIG: I adore the decor, it's very ornate.

FARMER: I can't tell.

PIG: We've been sitting here long enough.

FARMER: It's not important.

PIG: Just shoot me now.

FARMER adjusts his rifle, prepares for the shot.

PIG, now dead from the neck down, her black grape in brine.

B l a c k o u t .

E N D

Good Bone

a good bone broth disorients.
a good bone broth makes what's dead more
dead & erases the animal that once was
from memory. a good bone broth brews

in your mouth as you read this. you can feel it
collect in almost-cavities, simmering
on low heat. your teeth, perfectly
sized ladles. a good bone broth is

distance. with the flesh peeled back
there's room to indulge in what once was.
your mouth knows the final set of molars
pay homage to the animal.

you smile: it's the closest you get to being
outside yourself. your wisdom teeth are
anything but, but they are
bouillon cubes, cleaving.

i hear a dentist becomes a dentist when he fails culinary school.

What Is Above an Oven of This Proportion?

A woman dressed for domesticity falls
for the glamour of a late-night infomercial.

The SubZero Wolf Oven holds its showroom
at pedestal height, the crown jewel
of the functionalist kitchen.

She expels the home—the emptiness she finds
filling in its own way

couch table   couch table   couch   no island but a single
shelving unit   no granite but marble no
                                contact paper   please
contact a representative.

And still short she
slices her tongue to sell. She
prepares a six-hour goulash

a harbinger of matrimonial bliss but
dinners are apocalyptic by nature.
She can taste absolutely nothing!

The tiny tech screws loosen
more so than her own. The Wolf
& her mouth poorly wired,
the goulash rubber-raw. And tasting
absolutely nothing
she's dressed for a funeral.

Calories Burnt in Death Rattle

Generations of dust cling
to the building blocks
left to fester from when
Mad Cow ran rampant
& my mother stopped
trusting my pocket depth.

Rot won't shatter, rot
does shield. What's left
to eat—what's edible?

What's edible—my digestion
forgoes commas.

My best math deals
in imaginaries. I make room
for uncalorics! make time
for still swallows!

Anything fits now
in these orifices:
the house, my bowels.

The Butcher Courts a Bull Dyke

When several forms of deli meat conflate
the butcher knows his mother likes to watch.
Avoiding steel, the butcher bends to take
in lieu of pay, a patron's thrusting crotch.
She squats in corners pressed upon her heel.
Obscene, her knees give out just short of prayer.
Her son, the butcher, blesses every meal,
no matter what or whom begets the fare.
In jest *What leaden ego-meat you have!*
Ingest it still, she will, or else confront
the raw & rising heat of slaughtered calf.
Traversing fit & proper, primal grunts
belay. The damned butcher courts a dyke
reminding him all women are alike.

HOMEBODY VLOG / THE ALL-GIRLS DREAM

faceless, i learn   her through laughter
& unpainted toes. i'm a slut for repetition
                              (just look at my black book)
so routine drew me in. once

she mentioned illness, the one all girls dream
of—
         & i resumed the armchair. 3,000 calories a day to maintain
yourself. settling into velvet
upholstery, she drinks   herself to
completion: lemonade & iced coffee. a three-pot stew follows

& a question: how long
have you been alone? 8 years. how many times
have you moved? 3. why? better left
unsaid.
              but her laughter!

i'm not the only one tuning in   / not the only one ignoring her
facelessness / not
the only one who lets her laugh curl through space/
white noise.

she goes to the market to the café to buy summer-weight pajamas to the park
to the trash bins downstairs. she photographs her walks on an instant camera
& retreats to the studio, shows us her grocery haul. she orders pizza or fried
chicken or hair dryer or tteokbokki or vintage lampshade or neutral weave
sofa or bedside table or summer-weight pajamas because the store didn't have
the color she wanted: red.

how long have you been alone? i'm not
alone now. how many times
have you moved? 3. why? to be
alone. i'm familiar with her wrist circumference
         when she cooks. i hold my arm up to the screen
for reference. i try to follow similar
body types. the only thing about her
that's heavy: grocery orders. 3,000
calories a day to maintain herself: the illness
                              all girls dream of.

she captions her videos & i'm a diligent reader. i read into her afternoon naps & fear she's dying. i
fear her 8 years of living alone is 26 of loneliness. i fear her laugh is crackle, flint for a house fire. i'm
posturing, sure.   have you ever met a routine that didn't break you?

R. Stempel is a genderqueer Ukrainian-Jewish poet and PhD student in English literature at SUNY-Binghamton. They received their MFA in Poetry from Adelphi University. They are the author of the chapbook, *Interiors* (Foundlings Press, 2022), and their work has recently appeared in *Jet Fuel Review, Gulf Coast Magazine,* and *Hobart.* At one point, they held the second highest score in *Aliens: Armageddon* at the Chinatown Fair Family Fun Center in New York City. Find them at https://www.racheljstempel.com/.

www.ingramcontent.com/pod-product-compliance
Lightning Source LLC
LaVergne TN
LVHW041510070426
835507LV00012B/1472